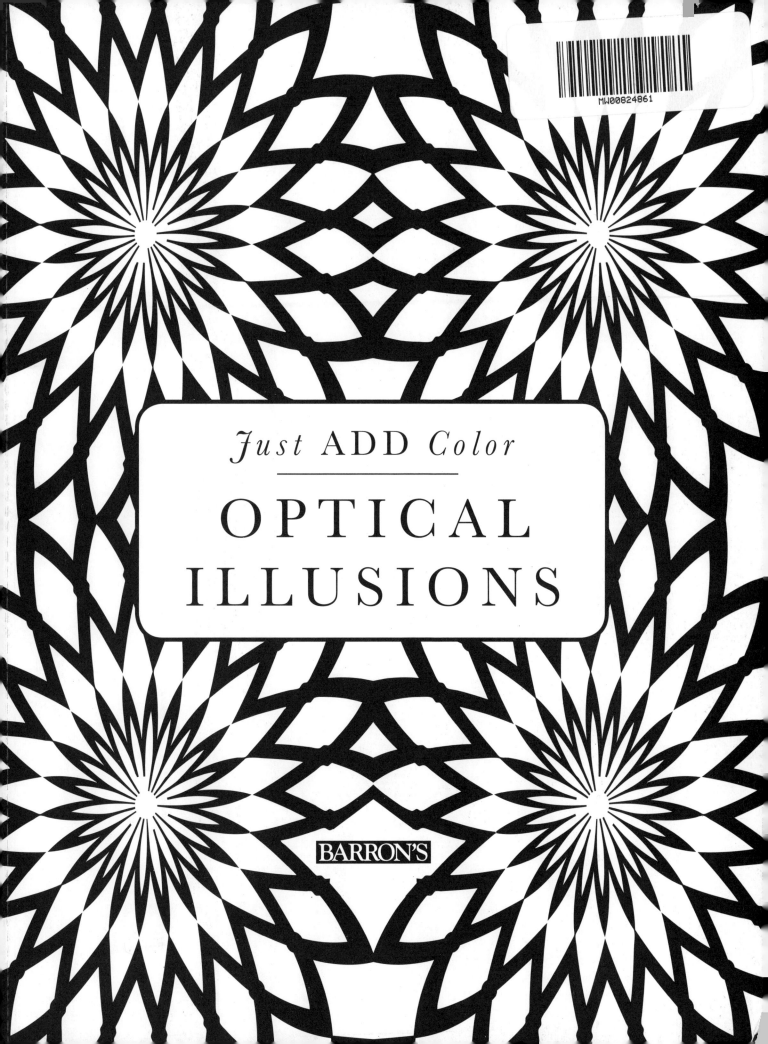

Just ADD *Color*

OPTICAL
ILLUSIONS

BARRON'S

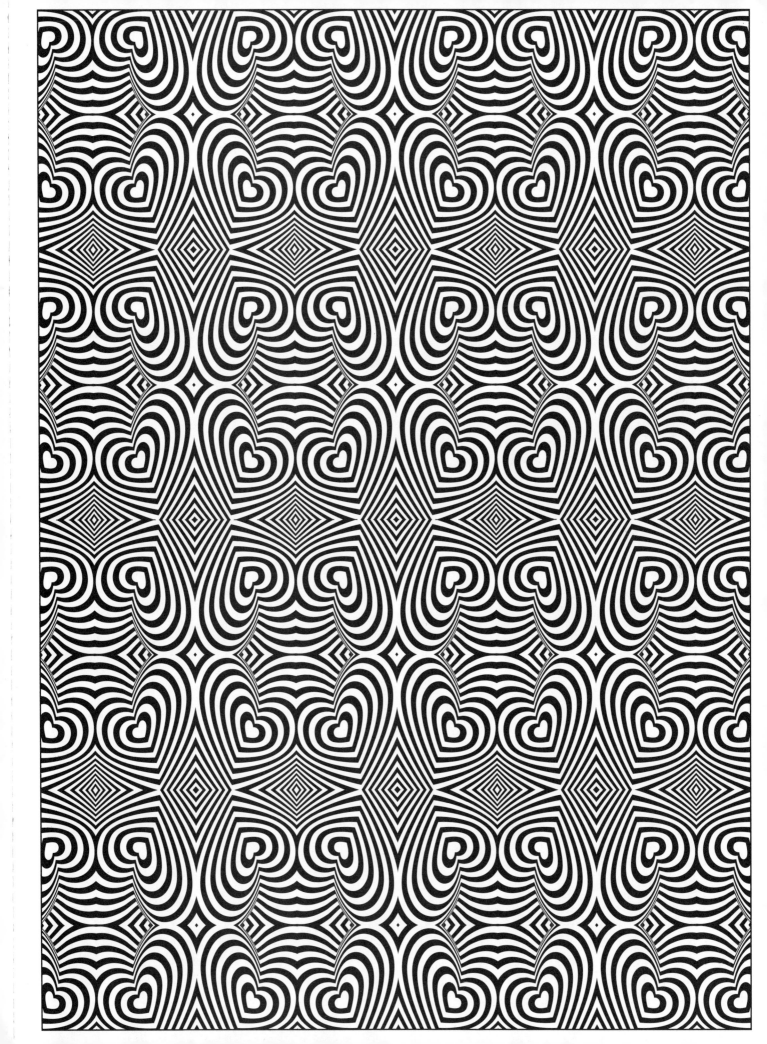

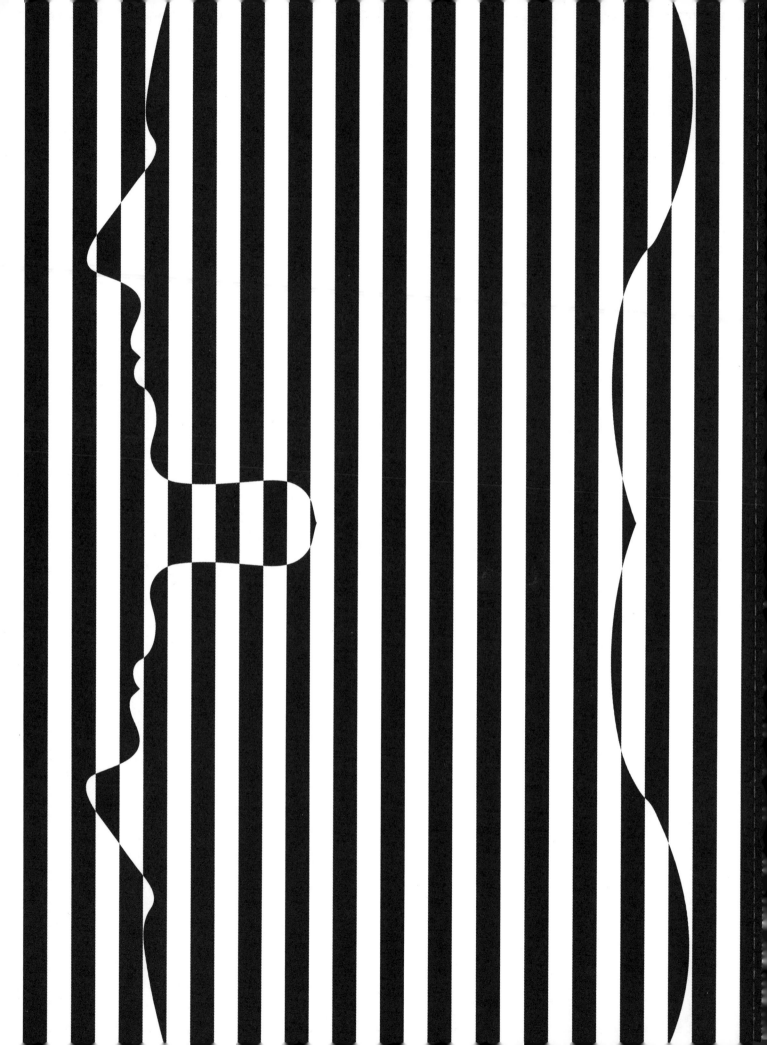

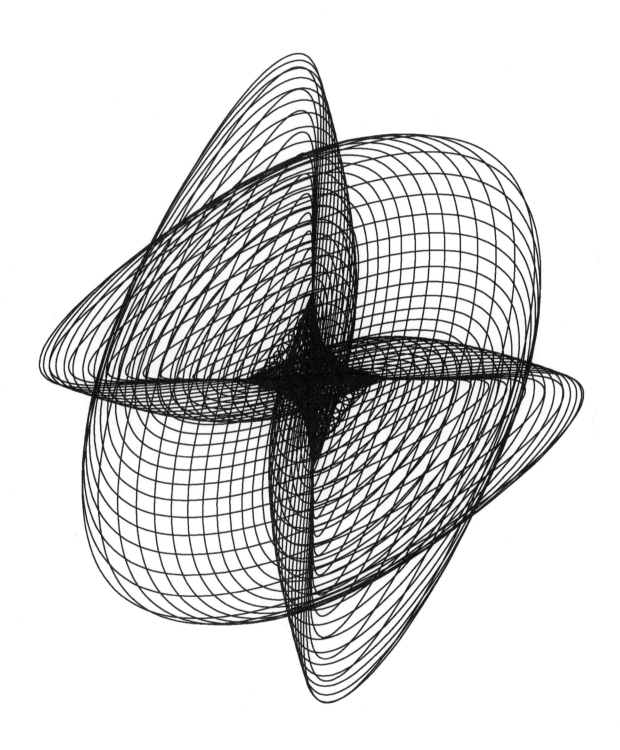

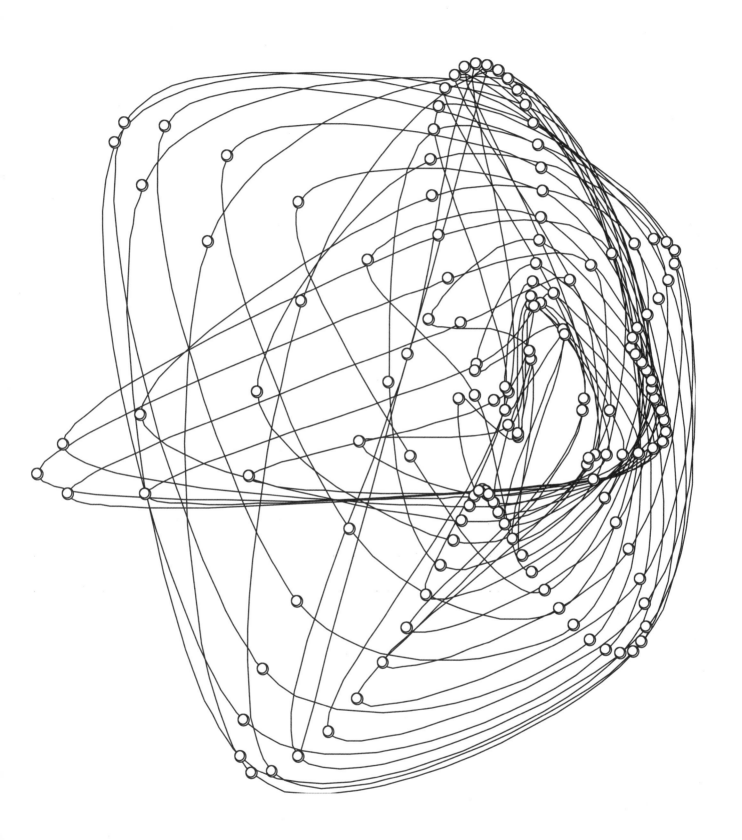

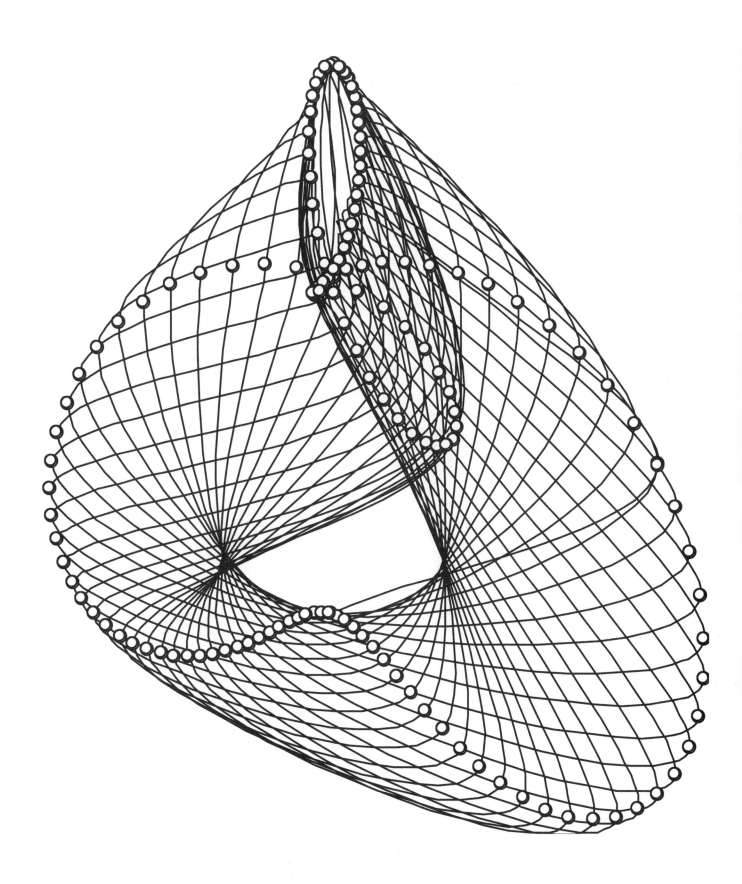

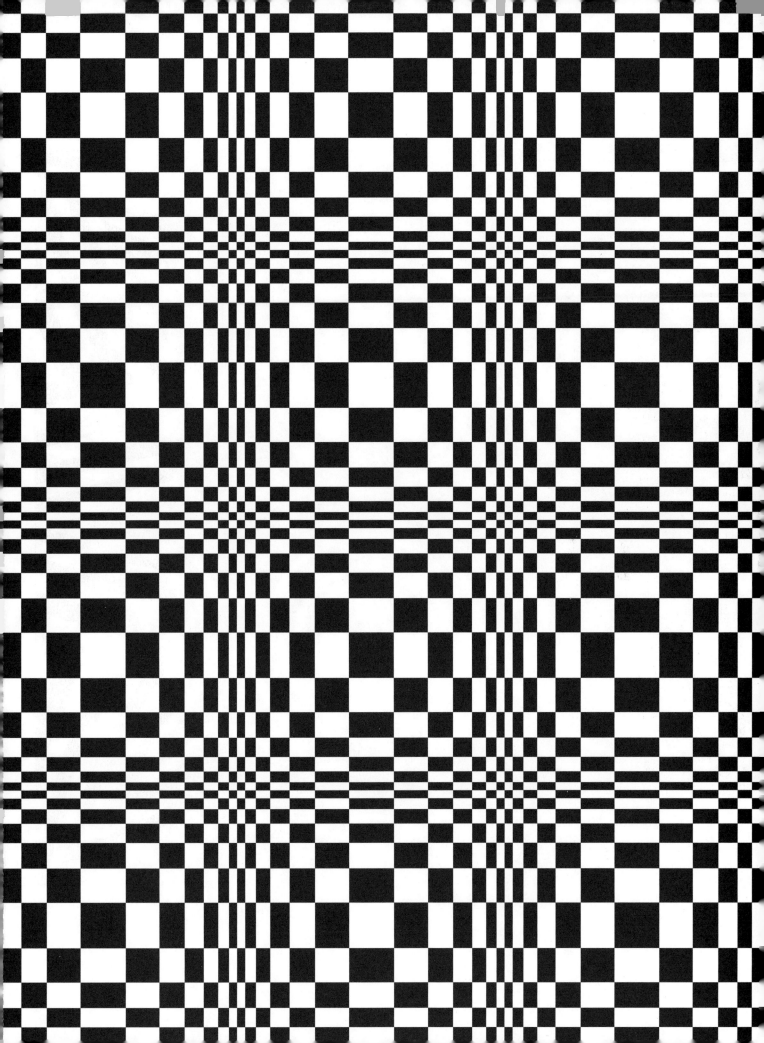

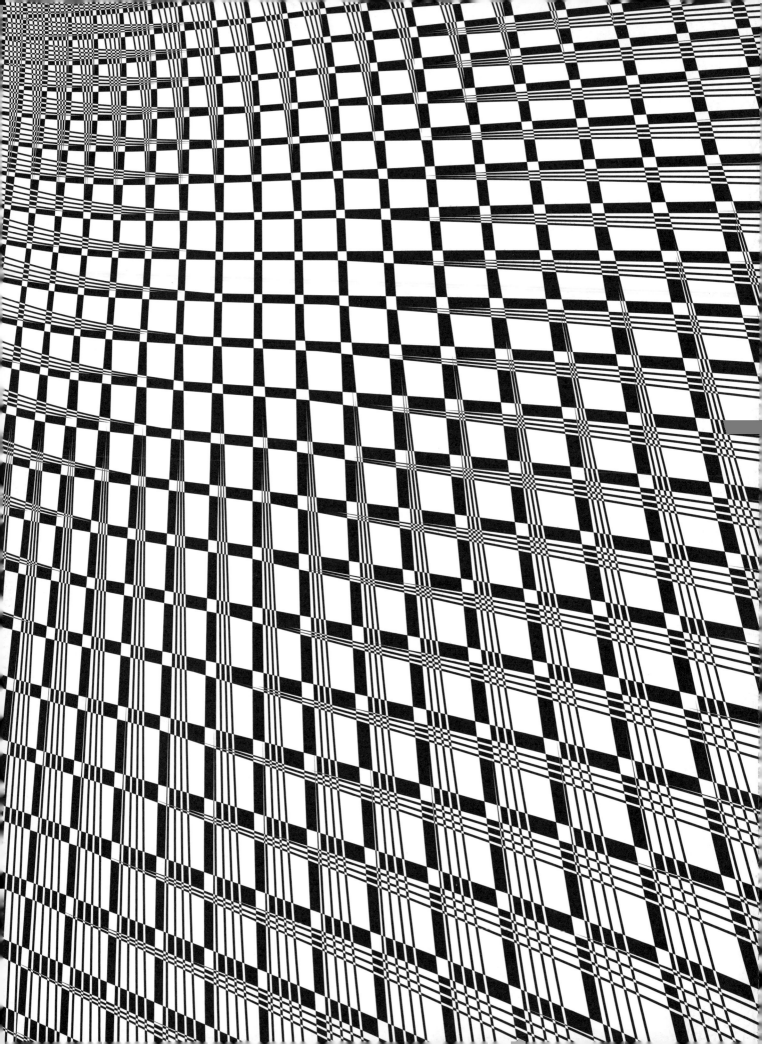

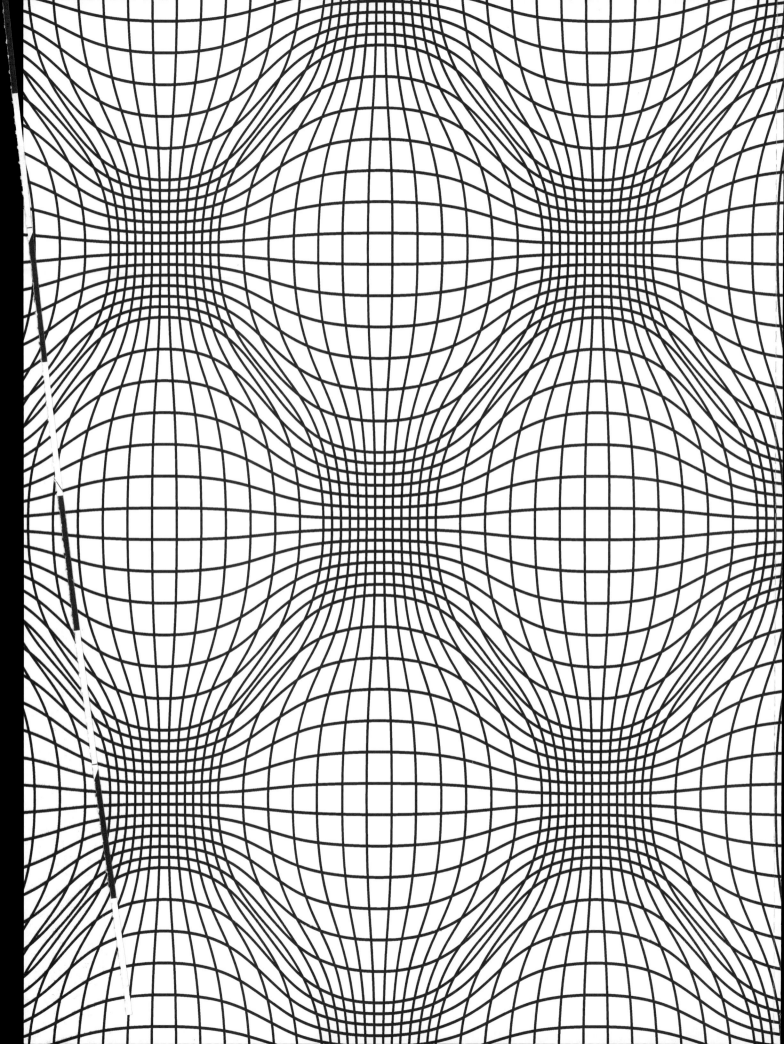

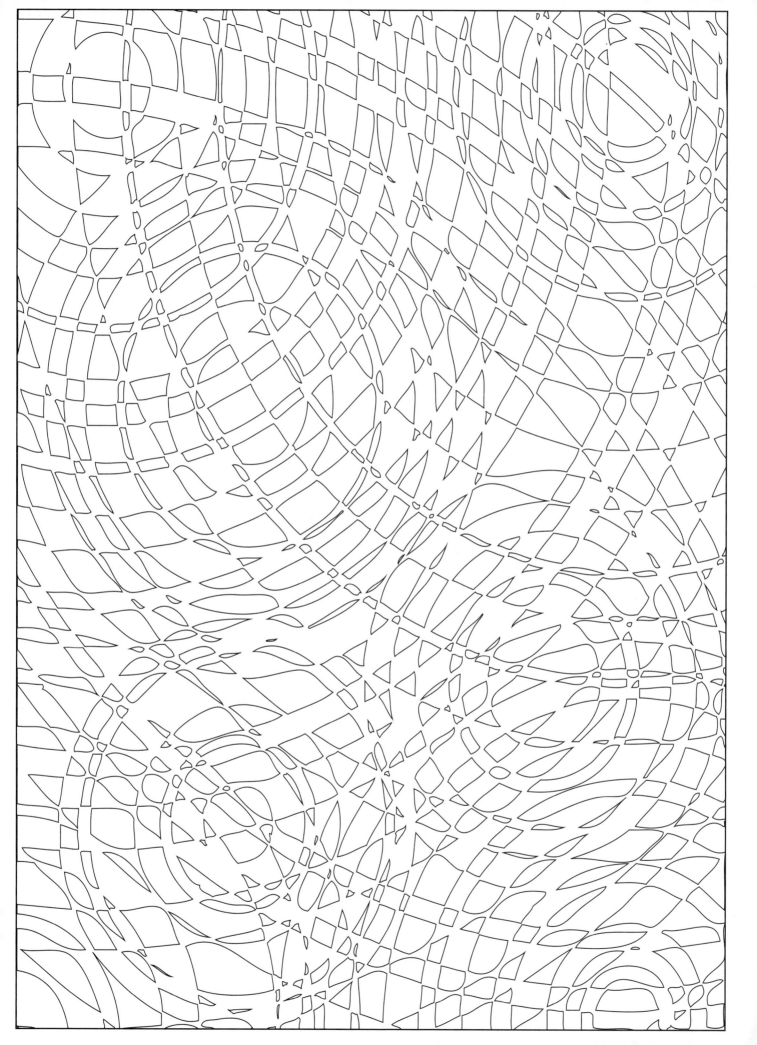

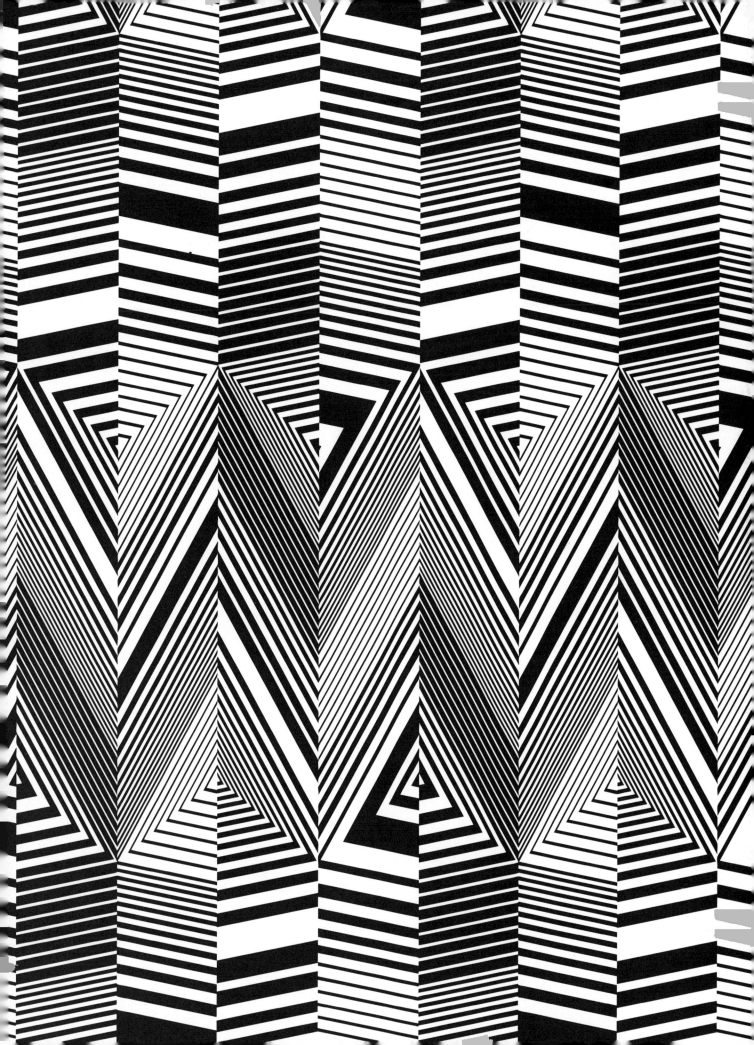

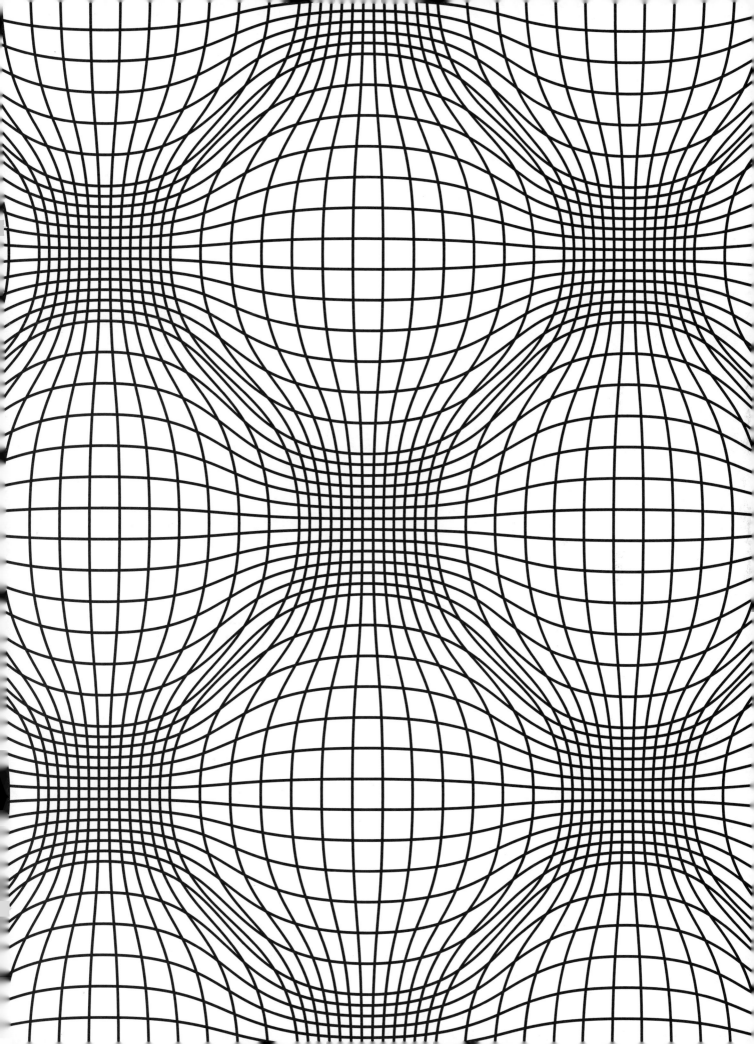

First edition for North America published in 2015 by Barron's Educational Series, Inc.

© Copyright 2015 by Carlton Publishing Group.

All inquiries should be addressed to:

Barron's Educational Series, Inc.
250 Wireless Boulevard,
Hauppauge, New York 11788
www.barronseduc.com

ISBN: 978-1-4380-0612-3

Library of Congress Control Number: 2014939398

Manufactured by Marquis, Louiseville, Canada

Printed in Canada

9 8 7 6 5 4

Picture credits: Shutterstock and Thinkstock

For best results, colored pencils are recommended.